TABLE OF CONTENTS

Novel-Ties® are printed on recycled paper.

Copyright © 2002, 2003, 2015 by LEARNING LINKS

For the Teacher

This reproducible study guide consists of instructional material to use in conjunction the book *Because of Winn-Dixie*. Written in chapter-by-chapter format, the guide contains a synopsis, pre-reading activities, vocabulary and comprehension exercises, as well as extension activities to be used as follow-up to the novel.

NOVEL-TIES are either for whole class instruction using a single title or for group instruction where each group uses a different novel appropriate to its reading level. Depending upon the amount of time allotted to it in the classroom, each novel, with its guide and accompanying lessons, may be completed in two to four weeks.

The first step in using NOVEL-TIES is to distribute to each student a copy of the novel and a folder containing all of the duplicated worksheets. Begin instruction by selecting several pre-reading activities in order to set the stage for the reading ahead. Vocabulary exercises for each chapter always precede the reading so that new words will be reinforced in the context of the book. Use the questions on the chapter worksheets for class discussion or as written exercises.

The benefits of using NOVEL-TIES are numerous. Students read good literature in the original, rather than in abridged or edited form. The good reading habits formed by practice in focusing on interpretive comprehension and literary techniques will be transferred to the books students read independently. Passive readers become active, avid readers.

SYNOPSIS

Ten-year-old India Opal Buloni and her father, a preacher, have just moved to the little town of Naomi, Florida, where they live in a trailer park. Since the only children close in age are the pesty Dewberry brothers and the pinch-faced Amanda Wilkinson, India Opal is lonely. Her mother left home seven years before, and her father spends most of his time preparing sermons for his church. The preacher never talks about his wife's abandonment of her family, and this makes India Opal feel even lonelier.

Life begins to improve when India Opal adopts a stray dog running loose in the Winn-Dixie grocery store. She saves the dirty, shaggy dog from the pound by claiming it as her own and worries that her father will not allow her to keep it.

For once, luck is on India Opal's side. The dog she has decided to call Winn-Dixie is permitted to join the family. After a bath and some grooming, the dog charms everyone in town. He is the perfect pet except for his pathological fear of thunder.

Because of Winn-Dixie, Opal gets to know Miss Franny Block, the librarian who tells her wonderful stories about the past of this small southern town. The dog also helps his mistress get a job at Gertrude's Pets, where a sad-faced musician named Otis plays his guitar to soothe the animals. Ignoring the warnings of the Dewberry brothers, India Opal even dares to befriend Gloria Dump, an elderly woman who is rumored to be a witch.

India Opal longs for friends her own age. During this eventful summer, she actually learns to appreciate unhappy Amanda and is invited to Sweetie Pie Thomas's sixth birthday party. When India Opal and Gloria decide to host their own celebration, all these new friends come. Even the Dewberry boys find their way onto the guest list.

The party begins happily, with decorations and fruit punch and sandwiches. But suddenly, a thunderstorm blows up, terrifying Winn-Dixie. The dog disappears, and a heart-broken India Opal and her father set out to find him in the rain. Finally, they must accept that he may be gone forever, just like India Opal's wonderful mother. Father and daughter learn that sometimes, you simply have to let go of love.

All ends well when Winn-Dixie is found cowering under Gloria's bed. As the party guests gather around Otis's guitar to sing, India Opal Buloni is no longer the lonely new girl in town. It turns out that she, too, has a knack for making friends.

PRE-READING QUESTIONS AND ACTIVITIES

1. Preview the book by reading the title and the author's name and looking at the illustration on the cover. What do you think the book will be about? Do you think it takes place in the city or the country? Will it be a story about real life or is it a fantasy? Have you read any other books by the same author?

2. **Cooperative Learning Activity:** This story explores how friendships begin and grow. Work with a small group of classmates to list and discuss ways people can become friends. Think about the ingredients that go into a friendship. As you read the novel, notice how India Opal gets to know people in the community.

3. In this novel, a character makes a list of ten special things about another person. Think of a person you love. Make a list of ten qualities that make this person unique and special to you.

4. **Social Studies Connection:** This story is set in rural Florida. Do some research to find out about this part of the United States. What is the climate and geography of the region? You might find this information in an atlas or encyclopedia, or on the Internet.

5. If you were to have a party just to celebrate friendship, how many people would you invite? Would the people be only your age or all ages? What would you plan to do at the party? What food might you serve?

6. The main character in this story is curious about other people. She asks questions to find out what she wants to know. Make a list of interview questions you could ask someone whom you do not know well. Then interview a classmate and record his or her responses on paper.

7. Do you have a pet? Have you ever wanted a pet? Imagine that you are trying to convince a parent that you should have a dog for a pet. Make a list of the reasons for and against having this kind of pet. Of course, list more reasons in the "For" column.

Reasons For Having a Dog	**Reasons Against Having a Dog**

8. As you read *Because of Winn-Dixie*, fill in the story map on the following page.

STORY MAP

Title _____

Author _____

Main Characters	Descriptions
India Opal	
The Preacher	
Winn-Dixie	
Miss Franny Block	
Gloria Dump	
Otis	

Plot—Main Events

First, _____

_____

_____

Then, _____

_____

_____

Next, _____

_____

_____

Finally, _____

_____

_____

Theme—Message

This story taught me that _____

_____

_____

CHAPTERS 1–4

Vocabulary: Draw a line from each word on the left to its definition on the right. Then use the numbered words to fill in the blanks in the sentences below.

1. sermon
2. concerned
3. orphan
4. fortunate
5. produce
6. constellation

a. lucky
b. fruits and vegetables
c. worried
d. group of stars
e. child whose parents have both died
f. speech with a religious lesson, usually given by a member of the clergy

. . . .

1. When Miguel found a winning lottery ticket, he felt _____ indeed.

2. Since I needed apples to bake a pie, I went to the _____ section of the supermarket.

3. My cousin came to live with my family after she became a(n) _____.

4. The Big Dipper is the easiest _____ to find in the sky.

5. When I heard the preacher's _____ about brotherly love, I thought he knew that I had just had a fight with my brother Jim.

6. Our teacher was _____ by the loud buzzing of wasps at the open windows.

> Read to find out whether India Opal can keep Winn-Dixie.

Questions:

1. Why did India Opal tell the store manager that the stray dog belonged to her?

2. Why did India Opal think of her father as "the preacher"?

3. How did India Opal get her unusual name?

4. Why did India Opal think that her father might let her keep Winn-Dixie?

5. What did India Opal mean when she said that she and the dog were "almost like orphans?"

Chapters 1–4 (cont.)

Questions for Discussion:

1. Why do you suppose the preacher let India Opal keep the stray dog? What did this show about him?

2. Why do you imagine India Opal talked so much to her new pet?

3. What do you think India Opal learned about her mother from the ten things her father told her? How did this information make her feel about her missing parent?

Literary Devices:

I. *Simile* — A simile is a figure of speech in which two words are compared using the words "like" or "as." For example:

> Mostly, he looked like a big piece of old brown carpet that had been left out in the rain.

What is being compared?

_____

What does this tell you about the appearance of the stray dog?

_____

II. *Metaphor* — A metaphor is an implied or suggested comparison. For example:

> I could see him [India Opal's father] pulling his old turtle head back into his stupid turtle shell.

What is being compared?

_____

What does this reveal about India Opal's father? And what does it reveal about Opal's feelings about her father?

_____

_____

_____

III. *Hyperbole* — Hyperbole is a figure of speech in which there is an intentional exaggeration. For example:

> She [India Opal's mother] liked to plant things. She had a talent for it. She could stick a tire in the ground and grow a car.

Why do you think India Opal's father used hyperbole?

_____

_____

Chapters 1–4 (cont.)

IV. *Point of View* — Point of view in literature refers to the person who is telling a story. We learn about people and events through this person's eyes. The story may be narrated by a character in the story (first-person narrative) or by the author (third-person narrative).

From whose point of view is this story told?

_____

Why do you think the author chose this point of view?

_____

_____

Writing Activities:

1. Imagine that you are India Opal and write a letter to your mother that tells about life in Friendly Corners Trailer Park. What do you think that India Opal would most want her mother to know?

2. Suppose that India Opal decided to make a poster about the homeless dog. Write a description of Winn-Dixie. Make your description so detailed and precise that someone could easily identify the dog. You may illustrate the poster with your own drawing or a picture you find in a magazine. Use the space below or a large piece of card stock to create your poster.

LOST DOG

CHAPTERS 5–9

Vocabulary: Synonyms are words with similar meanings. Draw a line from each word in column A to its synonym in column B. Then use the words in column A to fill in the blanks in the sentences below.

	A		B
1.	talent	a.	same
2.	embarrassed	b.	remember
3.	identical	c.	humiliated
4.	irritating	d.	disregard
5.	ignore	e.	capability
6.	recall	f.	annoying

. . . .

1. It was hard to concentrate on my homework because of my brother's _____ habit of drumming on the table.

2. I felt _____ when I tripped and fell as I walked across the stage.

3. The photograph helped me _____ the events and the people at your birthday party three years ago.

4. Since everyone in my family has musical _____, it is expected that I will sing or play an instrument.

5. It is better to _____ your sister's teasing than to fight with her.

6. The twins preferred to wear different clothing rather than the _____ outfits their mother chose.

> Read to learn how India Opal begins to make new friends.

Chapters 5–9 (cont.)

Questions:

1. Why did India Opal decide that Winn-Dixie could no longer be left outside on a leash?

2. How was the Open Arms Baptist Church different from most other churches?

3. Why was India Opal lonely, even with Winn-Dixie for company?

4. What problem did India Opal think she had in common with Miss Franny Block?

5. Why did some of the neighborhood children think that Gloria Dump was a witch?

6. Why did Otis give India Opal a job in his pet store?

Questions for Discussion:

1. What evidence revealed that the preacher had a good sense of humor?

2. In what ways do you think Winn-Dixie was making India Opal's life happier?

3. What do you imagine Gloria Dump meant when she told India Opal that she had to rely on her heart?

Literary Devices:

I. *Simile* — What is being compared in the following simile?

Winn-Dixie looked like a furry bullet, shooting across the building, chasing that mouse.

_____

Why is this passage better than saying, "Winn-Dixie ran fast"?

_____

_____

II. *Hyperbole* — Find an example of hyperbole in the first sentence of Chapter Seven. Write it on the line below.

_____

Why do you think storytellers often use hyperbole?

_____

_____

Chapters 5–9 (cont.)

III. *Irony* — Irony of situation refers to the difference between what is expected and what really exists.

What is ironic about the sign in the pet shop window?

_____

_____

Science Connection:

Do some research to learn about the palmetto trees that once grew wild in Florida. Find a picture of this tree and display it in your classroom.

Language Study: Idioms

An idiom is an expression that does not mean exactly what it says. For example, the statement, "It is raining cats and dogs," actually means it is raining very hard. Tell what each of the following idioms really means.

1. Getting left behind probably <u>made his heart feel empty</u>.

_____

_____

2. I had <u>my nose stuck in a book</u>.

_____

_____

Writing Activity:

Write about a time when you experienced loneliness. Tell why you felt that way and what you did to try to end your feelings of loneliness. Were you successful? What advice would you give to someone who feels lonely?

CHAPTERS 10–13

Vocabulary: Analogies are equations in which the first pair of words has the same relationship as the second pair of words. For example, DARK is to LIGHT as MERRY is to GLUM. Both pairs of words are opposites. Choose the best word from the Word Box to complete each of the analogies below.

```
                        WORD BOX
        amazed      pathological      terrorized
        ignorant    refresh
```

1. PUNY is to ROBUST as _____ is to KNOWLEDGEABLE.

2. _____ is to ASTONISHED as TOWERING is to HIGH.

3. WATER is to _____ as FOOD is to NOURISH.

4. CONCERNED is to CARING as FRIGHTENED is to _____.

5. NORMAL is to _____ as TORN is to WHOLE.

> Read to find out how India Opal makes new friends.

Questions:

1. What can you tell about Gloria Dump from her response to India Opal's stories?

2. What was the joke that the preacher and Winn-Dixie shared?

3. How did the preacher explain Winn-Dixie's odd behavior during the thunderstorm?

4. Why did Otis sometimes let the animals out of their cages?

5. Why did Sweetie Pie Thomas think that Otis had magic powers?

Questions for Discussion:

1. Why do you suppose Gloria Dump had India Opal plant a tree in her garden?

2. Do you agree with Gloria Dump that the Dewberry boys teased India Opal because they really wanted to make friends with her?

3. How do you imagine the preacher would have reacted if he knew that Otis had served time in prison?

Chapters 10–13 (cont.)

Science Connection:

There is evidence that music can affect the mood or behavior of people, animals, and even plants. Do some research to learn about experiments involving music. Find out how some kinds of music may help us to learn, cheer up, or relax. Share your findings with a group of your classmates.

Literary Element: Vernacular

A writer may use vernacular, the nonstandard language of a place or group, to show how people actually speak. For example:

"Hmmph," said Gloria Dump. "I ain't going nowhere. I be right here."

Dialogue like this makes characters seem real to us. What other examples of vernacular can you find in this part of the story? Who is speaking?

_____

_____

_____

Writing Activity:

India Opal tells some stories about the adventures she shares with Winn-Dixie. What adventure of your own would you like to share with others? Write a story about something surprising or exciting that has happened to you or to someone you know.

CHAPTERS 14–18

Vocabulary: Antonyms are words with opposite meanings. Draw a line from each word in column A to its antonym in column B. Then use the words in column A to fill in the sentences below.

A	B
1. adult	a. aggravate
2. harsh	b. joyous
3. comfort	c. gentle
4. hero	d. serious
5. melancholy	e. child
6. idle	f. villain

. . . .

1. The sound of soft music will always _____ me when I am upset.

2. I became _____ after my dog ran away.

3. With only one day to finish my work, I have no time for _____ chatter.

4. If you want to swim at the lake, be sure a(n) _____ is present.

5. The firefighter became a(n) _____ to my family after saving us from a fire in our home.

6. If you move to Alaska, you can expect winters to be long and _____.

> Read to find out how India Opal's number of friends is growing.

Questions:

1. What advice did Gloria Dump give India Opal about judging others?

2. Why did Gloria Dump take Opal out to see her special tree?

3. Why did India Opal want to read a story to Gloria Dump?

4. Why had Littmus K. Block decided to build a candy factory?

Chapters 14–18 (cont.)

5. What did Amanda Wilkinson and India Opal have in common?

6. How did the lessons India Opal learned from Gloria and Miss Franny change her attitude toward the Dewberry brothers?

7. What helped India Opal to better understand Amanda?

Questions for Discussion

1. Do you think Gloria gave India Opal good advice?

2. Although the Littmus Lozenge was fiction, have you ever experienced something that was both happy and sad at the same time?

3. Why do you suppose Miss Franny recommended the book *Gone With the Wind* for India Opal to read to Gloria Dump?

Social Studies Connection:

Do some research to learn about the Civil War. Use an encyclopedia, textbook, or the Internet to get the facts about how this conflict began and what its long-lasting effects were. Prepare an oral report and present it to a group of your classmates.

Literary Device: Cliffhanger

A cliffhanger is a device borrowed from serialized silent films in which an episode ended at a moment of great suspense or tension. In a book, it usually appears at the end of a chapter to encourage the reader to continue on in the book. What is the cliffhanger at the end of Chapter Sixteen?

_____

_____

Writing Activities:

1. Write about a time when you felt that you were judged unfairly. Describe the issue that caused the judgment and tell what happened. Do you feel that the other person finally began to understand you?

2. Imagine that you are Amanda Wilkinson. Write a diary entry telling how you felt as you sat with India Opal and listened to Miss Franny's story about Littmus K. Block and the Civil War.

CHAPTERS 19–23

Vocabulary: Use the words from the Word Box and the clues below to complete the crossword puzzle.

WORD BOX				
ache	arrested	convinced	guitar	squawk
amuse	complicated	decorate	nervous	theme

Across

2. persuaded
5. seized; taken into custody by the police
6. cry out harshly
7. string musical instrument, usually strummed
8. main idea; subject

Down

1. feel pain
2. difficult; complex
3. uneasy; fearful
4. adorn or make pretty with ornaments
5. entertain

Read to find out why India Opal decides to have a party.

Chapters 19–23 (cont.)

Questions:

1. What was the real reason that Otis had gone to jail?

2. Why did Gloria laugh when she learned how Otis broke the law?

3. Why did India Opal decide to have a party?

4. Why did the preacher say in his blessing that "We appreciate the complicated and wonderful gifts you give us in each other"?

5. Why did India Opal think the Dewberry brothers might not come to the party?

6. Why did India Opal run out in the rain?

Questions for Discussion:

1. In your opinion, why did Gloria Dump insist that India Opal invite the Dewberry brothers to the party?

2. Why do you think Otis didn't agree to come to the party when India Opal first invited him?

3. Do you think Otis deserved to be jailed for his behavior?

4. If someone gave you a Littmus Lozenge, how would it taste?

5. Do you think India Opal should feel guilty about Winn-Dixie's disappearance?

Cooperative Learning Activity:

Work with a small group of your classmates to create a simple party menu. Write down a recipe for one of the foods on your list. Share this recipe with the rest of your class. Then you might want to have a Winn-Dixie party in your own classroom to celebrate friendship.

Writing Activities:

1. India Opal read aloud to Gloria because she wanted to do something nice for her. Have you ever done a special favor for a friend? Write a journal entry describing the circumstances.

2. Pretend you are a newspaper reporter in the small town of Naomi. Write a brief news article about the party held at Gloria Dump's house. Include the names of the guests and other important details about the social event.

CHAPTERS 24–26

Vocabulary: Use a word from the Word Box to replace the underlined word or phrase in each of the sentences below. Write the word on the line below the sentence.

```
                        WORD BOX
          drizzle      hymns       potions
          exist        platter     wad
```

1. Mother placed the roast turkey on her best <u>large serving plate</u>.

   _____

2. Trolls, fairies, and elves <u>are found</u> only in storybooks.

   _____

3. The witch mixed her <u>magical drinks</u> in an old rusty cauldron.

   _____

4. The teacher told the student to spit out his <u>small soft mass</u> of gum.

   _____

5. The choir sang some lovely <u>songs of praise or joy</u> this morning.

   _____

6. The <u>fine, steady drops</u> suddenly changed to a hard, pounding rain.

   _____

> Read to find out what happens at the party.

Questions:

1. How did India Opal occupy her mind while she searched for Winn-Dixie? Why did she do this?

2. Why did the preacher begin to cry while he was searching for Winn-Dixie?

3. How did the preacher and India Opal manage to comfort each other?

4. Why were the people invited to the party able to enjoy themselves while India Opal was searching for her dog?

5. Why was India Opal's party a success even though she was absent for most of it?

Chapters 24–26 (cont.)

Questions for Discussion:

1. Do you agree with Gloria that "you can only love what you got while you got it"?

2. Why do you suppose the possible loss of Winn-Dixie was so painful to India Opal and her father?

3. What helped the preacher and India Opal accept that India Opal's mother would not return to them?

4. Why do you think Dunlap Dewberry offered his hand to India Opal to help her up? Why do you think India Opal let him help her?

5. By the end of the story, how do you imagine India Opal felt about her new life in the town of Naomi?

6. Would you say that the preacher at the end of the story could still be compared to a turtle who hid in its shell?

Literary Device: Symbol

A symbol is an object, person, or event that represents an idea or set of ideas. What did Gloria's tree symbolize?

_____

_____

What did India Opal's tree symbolize?

_____

_____

Writing Activity:

Imagine you are India Opal and write a journal entry describing your thoughts and feelings about your life and the people in your life. Tell how you have changed since you first moved to Naomi.

CLOZE ACTIVITY

The following passage has been taken from Chapter Five of the novel. Read it through completely, and then fill in each blank with a word that makes sense. Afterwards you may compare your language with that of the author.

   Well, Winn-Dixie saw that mouse, and he was up and after him. One minute, everything was quiet and _____ [1] and the preacher was going on _____ [2] on and on; and the next _____,[3] Winn-Dixie looked like a furry bullet, _____ [4] across the building, chasing that mouse. _____ [5] was barking and his feet were _____ [6] all over the polished Pick-It-Quick floor, and people were clapping and hollering _____ [7] pointing. They really went wild when _____ [8] actually caught the mouse.

   "I have _____ [9] in my life seen a dog _____ [10] a mouse," said Mrs. Nordley. She _____ [11] sitting next to me.

   "He's a _____ [12] dog," I told her.

   "I imagine so," she said back.

   Winn-Dixie stood up _____ [13] in front of the whole church, _____ [14] his tail and holding the mouse _____ [15] careful in his mouth, holding onto _____ [16] tight but not squishing him.

   "I _____ [17] that mutt has got some retriever _____ [18] him," said somebody behind me. "That's _____ [19] hunting dog."

   Winn-Dixie took the mouse _____ [20] to the preacher and dropped it _____ [21] his feet. And when the mouse _____ [22] to get away, Winn-Dixie put his _____ [23] right on the mouse's tail. Then _____ [24] smiled up at the preacher. He _____ [25] him all his teeth. The preacher _____ [26] down at the mouse. He looked _____ [27] Winn-Dixie. He looked at me. He _____ [28] his nose. It got real quiet in _____ [29] Pick-It-Quick.

   "Let us pray," the preacher finally said, "for this mouse."

POST-READING ACTIVITIES

1. Return to the story map you began on page three of this study guide. Fill in additional information and compare your responses with those of your classmates.

2. Write a short sequel to *Because of Winn-Dixie*. Tell how India Opal's friendships with Amanda and the Dewberry brothers develop.

3. Make a list of ten special things you learned about India Opal. Include memorable things the character says and does, and add your own ideas and observations to the list.

4. Some authors give each chapter of a novel its own title. Write a title for each chapter of *Because of Winn-Dixie*.

5. In a story, a conflict is a struggle between opposing forces. In *Because of Winn-Dixie* India Opal must search for her dog in the midst of a frightening thunderstorm. This is an example of conflict between a person and nature. Many stories present more than one conflict. Use a chart, such as the one below, to list the conflicts explored in *Because Winn-Dixie*.

Type of Conflict	Example
person *vs.* person/society	
person *vs.* nature	
person *vs.* self (inner struggle)	

6. Except for the art on the cover, this book does not include illustrations. Draw a picture of one or more characters in the novel, based on the author's descriptions.

7. The characters in this book speak in the vernacular, the language of their region. Look back at the examples of vernacular you listed earlier in this study guide. Add to your list, skimming through the story to find more uses of regional or colorful language.

8. India Opal felt that Winn-Dixie was the ideal pet for her. What would your perfect pet be like? Draw a picture and write a description of this animal.

9. With the help of an adult, make your own party punch. Combine any fruits and juices you like to make a delicious drink for family and friends. Write the recipe and make copies to share with your classmates.

10. Imagine that this book is made into a movie. Who might play the roles of India Opal, the preacher, and the Dewberry boys? What scenes would you want to include, change, and omit? What would be the greatest challenge about making a film version of this book?

Post-Reading Activities (cont.)

11. **Literature Circle:** Have a literature circle discussion in which you tell your personal reactions to *Because of Winn-Dixie*. Here are some questions and sentence starters to help your literature circle begin a discussion.

    • Compare yourself to one of the characters in the book. How are you alike? How are you different?

    • Do any of the characters remind you of people that you know?

    • Do you find the characters in the book realistic? Why or why not?

    • Which character in the story is most like you? Why?

    • Which character do you like the most? The least?

    • What did you like best about the book? What did you like least?

    • Who else would you like to have read this book? Why?

    • What questions would you like to ask the author about this book?

    • I was worried when . . .

    • I was pleased when . . .

    • I laughed when . . .

    • I would have liked to see . . .

    • I wonder . . .

    • India Opal learned that . . .

    • I learned that . . .

SUGGESTIONS FOR FURTHER READING

* Armstrong, William. *Sounder*. HarperCollins.

* Burnford, Sheila. *The Incredible Journey*. Yearling.

   Byars, Betsy. *The Not-Just-Anybody Family*. Holiday House.

* Cleary, Beverly. *Dear Mr. Henshaw*. HarperCollins.

   _____. *Henry and Ribsy*. HarperCollins.

* Cone, Molly. *Mishmash*. Houghton Mifflin.

* Creech, Sharon. *Walk Two Moons*. HarperCollins.

   Estes, Eleanor. *The Middle Moffat*. Houghton Mifflin.

   Fleischman, Sid. *Jim Ugly*. Green Willow.

* Gipson, Fred. *Old Yeller*. Harper Perennial.

* Greene, Bette. *Philip Hall Likes Me, I Reckon Maybe*. Puffin.

* Holt, Kimberly Willis. *When Zachary Beaver Came to Town*. Square Fish.

* Paterson, Katherine. *Come Sing, Jimmy Jo*. Puffin.

* Paul, Christopher. *Bud, Not Buddy*. Laurel Leaf.

* Rawls, Wilson. *Where the Red Fern Grows*. Yearling.

* Rylant, Cynthia. *Missing May*. Scholastic.

* Taylor, Theodore. *The Trouble With Tuck*. Yearling.

Some Other Books by Kate DiCamillo

* *Flora and Ulysses*. Candlewick.

   The Magician's Elephant. Candlewick.

* *The Miraculous Journey of Edward Tulane*. Candlewick.

* *The Tale of Despereaux*. Candlewick.

* NOVEL-TIES Study Guides are available for these titles.

ANSWER KEY

Chapters 1–4

Vocabulary: 1. f 2. c 3. e 4. a 5. b 6. d; 1. fortunate 2. produce 3. orphan 4. constellation 5. sermon 6. concerned

Questions: 1. India Opal told the store manager that the stray dog belonged to her because she did not want it to be taken to the pound. 2. India Opal thought of her father as "the preacher" because he was usually busy preparing a sermon to deliver at church or preaching, or thinking about preaching. He seemed to spend more time preaching than being a parent. 3. India Opal got her unusual name because her father had once been a missionary in India; her middle name was the same as her grandmother's. 4. India Opal thought that her father might let her keep Winn-Dixie because he often reminded her that they should help those less fortunate than themselves: the dog was certainly less fortunate. 5. When India Opal said that she and the dog were "almost like orphans" she meant that neither of them had a mother nearby; her mother had left the family when India Opal was three years old.

Chapters 5–9

Vocabulary: 1. e 2. c 3. a 4. f 5. d 6. b; 1. irritating 2. embarrassed 3. recall 4. talent 5. ignore 6. identical

Questions: 1. India Opal decided that Winn-Dixie could no longer be kept outside on a leash because the dog howled unceasingly when it was left alone. This created a disturbance at the trailer park. 2. The Open Arms Baptist Church was different from most other churches because it had once been a convenience store, and because it had folding chairs for seating rather than pews. Altogether, it was a makeshift building with a congregation that permitted informalities in its worship services. 3. India Opal was lonely because she had recently moved to Naomi and did not know many people; particularly, she did not have a playmate her own age. 4. India Opal concluded that both she and Miss Franny Block suffered from loneliness. 5. Some of the neighborhood children thought that Gloria Dump was a witch for superficial reasons: her house was ramshackle, her yard was overgrown with weeds, and she did not keep up her appearance. 6. Otis decided to give India Opal a job in his pet store after Gertrude the parrot flew over and sat on Winn-Dixie's head, showing that she liked him. Also, his store was in dire need of someone to clean it and keep it neat.

Chapters 10–13

Vocabulary: 1. ignorant 2. amazed 3. refresh 4. terrorized 5. pathological

Questions: 1. From her response to India Opal's stories, you can tell that Gloria Dump was a good listener who had compassion and understanding for others. 2. The joke that the preacher and Winn-Dixie shared was that Winn-Dixie had never waited for the preacher's permission to sleep on Opal's bed. 3. The preacher explained that Winn-Dixie's odd behavior during the thunderstorm was the result of a pathological fear: a type of fear that could not be reasoned away. 4. Otis sometimes let the animals out of their cages so they could experience freedom: he knew what it was like to be locked up because he had spent some time in jail. 5. Sweetie Pie Thomas thought that Otis had magic powers because she had seen him charm the animals by playing his guitar for them.

Chapters 14–18

Vocabulary: 1. e 2. c 3. a 4. f 5. b 6. d; 1. comfort 2. melancholy 3. idle 4. adult 5. hero 6. harsh

Questions: 1. Gloria Dump advised India Opal not to judge people by what they had done in the past, but by their current behavior and attitudes. 2. Gloria Dump took India Opal to see her tree from which bottles were hanging to reveal her own tortured past when she had been an alcoholic. She didn't want India Opal to consider her own actions harshly nor the past actions of Otis and her mother. 3. India Opal wanted to read a story to Gloria Dump because Gloria's eyesight had become so bad, she could no longer read for herself. Also, she needed something to keep her occupied in order to keep the ghosts of her alcoholic past at bay. 4. After he returned home from his horrible experiences as a soldier in the Civil War and observed the death and destruction in his home, Littmus K. Block decided to build a candy factory to put some sweetness back into a war-torn world. 5. Both Amanda Wilkinson and India Opal shared experiences of sadness and loss. India Opal was sad over moving to a new community where she felt like an outsider and still suffered over her mother's abandonment. Amanda suffered over the loss of her brother who had died the year before. 6. The lessons India Opal learned from Gloria and Miss Franny made her more tolerant and kind toward the Dewberry brothers. 7. When the preacher told her

that little Carson Wilkinson had drowned last year, India Opal was better able to understand Amanda's sour attitude.

Chapters 19–23

Vocabulary: Across — 2. convinced 5. arrested 6. squawk 7. guitar 8. theme; Down — 1. ache 2. complicated 3. nervous 4. decorate 5. amuse

Questions: 1. The real reason Otis had gone to jail was that he struck and knocked out a policeman while resisting arrest for playing his guitar in a public place. 2. Gloria laughed when she learned how Otis broke the law because the story was so sad that it was funny; by "funny," she meant pathetic. 3. India Opal decided to have a party so that Otis could play his music in front of people and so that her new friends would be less lonely. 4. The preacher extolled the importance of friendship in his blessing because he believed that was the significance of the party. 5. India Opal thought the Dewberry brothers might not come to the party because they still feared that Gloria Dump was a witch. 6. India Opal ran out into the rain to find Winn-Dixie who had been forgotten and left outside when everyone ran indoors for cover. She worried that her neglect would cause the dog grief in a thunderstorm which she knew it feared.

Chapters 24–26

Vocabulary: 1. platter 2. exist 3. potions 4. wad 5. hymns 6. drizzle

Questions: 1. India Opal occupied her mind by creating a list of ten things she knew about Winn-Dixie. This activity kept up her spirits while she searched for her dog. It was also a way to remember Winn-Dixie in case he was not found. 2. The preacher began to cry because his daughter accused him of quitting on life, instead of searching for his wife in the past and searching for Winn-Dixie now. He was upset that his daughter did not understand that he loved his wife and loved Winn-Dixie. 3. The preacher and India Opal managed to comfort each other by expressing love and caring for one another. The preacher expressed his gratitude that his wife did not take India Opal with her. 4. The people at the party were able to enjoy Otis's music and each other because they had found Winn-Dixie hiding from the thunder under Gloria's bed. 5. India Opal's party was a success because everyone became good friends while they waited for her to return. Also, the preacher was able to express his love for his daughter as well as communicate with the others on a personal level.

NOTES